To Be Holy

Principles for Living the Spirit-filled Life

by
C. Neil Strait

Beacon Hill Press of Kansas City
Kansas City, Missouri

ISBN: 0-8341-0896-8

Printed in the United States of America

Cover Art: Royce Ratcliff

10   9   8   7   6   5   4   (1989)

To
JOLYNE

. . . whose interest in her father's work
is a constant challenge
and thrill!

Contents

Preface

The concept of the Spirit-filled life is nothing new to most who will be reading this book. Somewhere in the recent past you have probably read something about the Holy Spirit. It is a subject with growing interest. And, that is good! For the life of the church, and of the Christian, depends ultimately on what is understood about the Holy Spirit.

In searching for something fresh for my pulpit between Easter and Pentecost, I desired some new path over which I might take my people in pursuit of a deeper understanding of the Spirit-filled life. These chapters are the result of that study and that search.

What began as a seven-Sunday series, concluded 15 Sundays later. The use of an overhead projector allowed diagrams and illustrations that clarified concepts and ideas. What is a thrilling series for a pastor is not always so for laymen. I came upon a serendipity! As the end of the seven-sermon series approached, frequent requests came for me to continue. Now, anytime a preacher is asked to continue preaching on a theme, he's going to! I did, and it was a deepening time in our fellowship.

I offer these pages, not with the thought that there is anything new. I claim no theological expertise. Nearly all truths about the Holy Spirit have been expressed by the great preachers, the gifted scholars, or the gallant theologians. What I have tried to accomplish is to be very basic and practical about a great and thrilling subject. Sometimes we do not need the profound so much as we need a clarification of the practical. Amidst the pressures and perils of late 20th-century living, "practical" becomes an appealing word.

I must thank the congregation that I served, First Church of the Nazarene, Lansing, Mich., for allowing me freedom to share these truths with them. Their acceptance of my method and style was a challenge.

Special thanks are due to Mrs. Dale (Sharon) Folkert, who typed the manuscript, in the midst of keeping a busy district office running smoothly. There has to be a special grace and blessing in the economy of God for secretaries. One of God's special favors to me has been sending to me secretaries with graces and skills beyond the ordinary.

Let me affirm, at the beginning, my belief in the sanctified life. For over 20 years of ministry I have had occasion to study this truth, preach it, experience it, and see it work in the lives of people. That has been exciting in itself. I count it a privilege to be part of a church that believes in "proclaiming Christian holiness." May that day never come when we will hesitate to proclaim the "whole council of God" with respect to holiness. Faithfulness to this blessed truth makes our future certain. Failure to proclaim it makes our future cloudy.

As you read this book, keep watching for what God has planned for you. Your journey to holy living can be life's greatest journey. May it be so!

I send this volume forth with much faith—faith that God's Word is powerful, instructive, and strengthening.

Grand Rapids, Mich.   C. NEIL STRAIT

8

Introduction

In business there is an organizational principle that goes something like this:

- *Define the Objective:* define the mission/purpose with a stated objective.
- *Set Goals:* set targets toward which you can work to accomplish the objective. Define the steps to reach the objective.
- *Plan:* prepare a written procedure showing how you propose to accomplish the goals.
- *Organize:* organize your plan so it can be carried out quickly and completely. Identify the priorities.
- *Implement:* project your follow-through; that is, put the plan into action.
- *Control:* evaluate and re-align where necessary, to keep the organized plan on track.

In a nutshell—and in lay language—that's a procedure used by business and management. Needless to say, this is but a skeleton outline. Reams could be written about each of these. But, if this procedure is so important to the business executive and in management, why can't it be used in the spiritual realm? It can! And that is the thesis of this book.

This kind of organizational procedure has been used in an attempt to set down the various steps to the sanctified life and to see them in relation to a plan. We cannot entirely chart and formulate the work of the Spirit. It is not that easy. But we can focus on certain components that will help us to understand the whole process. Hopefully this approach will get at some practical truths regarding the sanctified life.

This study is targeted to the newer Christian. But, it is hoped that all might be helped—not because of what is written or the way it is written, but because old truths sometimes take on added meaning when presented in a different mode.

All of the facets of the Spirit-filled life are too numerous to cover in one book, so only the most important areas have been selected, keeping especially in mind those new to the terminology and experience of sanctification.

Chapter 1

Objective: To Be Holy

The objective for the one seeking the Spirit-filled life is simply this: *To Be Holy*. Five scriptures identify this objective as a biblical principle and as God's plan for our lives. They are:

• Ephesians 1:4 – "He chose us in him before the creation of the world to be holy and blameless in his sight."

• Romans 12:1 – "I urge you, brothers, in view of God's mercy, to offer your bodies as living sacrifices, holy and pleasing to God – which is your spiritual worship."

• Colossians 1:22 – "Now he has reconciled you by Christ's physical body through death to present you holy in his sight, without blemish and free from accusation."

• Colossians 3:12 – "As God's chosen people, holy and dearly loved, clothe yourselves with compassion, kindness, humility, gentleness and patience."

• 1 Peter 1:15-16 – "Just as he who called you is holy, so be holy in all you do; for it is written: 'Be holy, because I am holy.'"

John Wesley gave several scriptures supportive of the sanctified life. You may want to study these to get a better idea of the total picture. These scriptures are:

Ezekiel 36:25-27, 29	1 Thessalonians 5:23
Matthew 5:8	Titus 2:11-14
Matthew 5:48	Hebrews 6:1
Matthew 6:10	Hebrews 7:25
John 8:34-36	Hebrews 10:14
John 17:20-23	James 1:4
Romans 2:29	1 John 1:5
Romans 12:1	1 John 1:7
2 Corinthians 3:17-18	1 John 1:8-9
2 Corinthians 7:1	1 John 2:6
Galatians 2:20	1 John 3:3
Ephesians 3:14-19	1 John 3:8-10
Ephesians 5:27	1 John 5:13[1]
Philippians 3:15	

Now, the command/objective—"Be holy"—is admittedly a pretty tall order. No one will argue with that. And if a new Christian were confronted with this admonition right after getting up from the place of repentance, it would be mind-boggling, to say the least.

We need to remember that General Motors did not become a multi-billion-dollar corporation overnight. Back across the years men with vision and foresight sketched a pattern of growth through objectives, goal-setting, planning, organization, implementation, and control. What General Motors is today is the result of disciplined pursuit of an objective. And because they took it a step at a time, they arrived! Keep this principle in mind throughout this book.

The secret of the Spirit-filled life is *growth*, not just attainment! Before you take me to the heresy council, hear me out. The Spirit-filled life is—eventually—obtaining cleansing and Spirit-fulness. But where the crisis experience is seen as attainment, one can overlook the growing it takes to get there. By being faithful in implementing year after year, General Motors became a corporate giant. So, I contend that if we focus on the growth aspect, then the growing will take us to the obtainment, that is, to the point of making the complete consecration necessary to be entirely sanctified.

Definition

Let's take a look at the objective, "Be holy." The word *holy* means, among other things, "to be set apart." It means "belonging to the divine." Someone has said it is "living according to a spiritual system." Wesley said it is "doing what the holy law requires." Paul S. Rees points out that the root idea of the Hebrew word is "that of withdrawal and consecration: withdrawal from what is common or unclean, consecration to what is divine, sacred, pure."[2]

Adam Clarke said, "God is holy, and this is the eternal reason why all his people should be holy."[3] Clarke goes on to say, "From a simple, pure affection of love, he made man for the manifestation of his own perfections . . . that he might be made a partaker of his holiness and . . . his happiness."[4]

Deprogramming

Probably we do not need a definition of *holy* so much as we need to deprogram our thinking in regards to the word *holy*. We do not have nearly as hard a problem with the word and concept of *holy* as we do the interpretations and ideas that have been tacked onto it. So much of what we have heard about holiness and sanctification has given us a false or improper concept of God and the sanctified life. Misconceptions, misinterpretations, and misunderstandings surface and defenses go up all over the place.

Sometimes I have wished that there could be some kind of mental wastebasket at the entry to every sanctuary with a sign, "Discard your junk here!" Sometimes we bring into our study of the Spirit-filled life erroneous ideas that keep the heart from growing and responding to the Spirit's possibilities.

Develop

Another step in the objective is to develop a proper attitude—an attitude that is positive. If one is to approach such a demanding objective without fear of failure, he must have an attitude that believes holiness can be obtained. Just as attitude is decisive in every other area of development, it is crucial in our spiritual development. Growth, wherever it occurs, is dependent on attitude.

Lowell Peacock writes this about attitude, "Attitude is the first quality that marks the successful man. If he has a positive attitude and is a positive thinker who likes challenges and difficult situations, then he has half his success achieved. On the other hand, if he is a negative thinker who is narrow-minded and refuses to accept new ideas and has a defeatist attitude, he hasn't got a chance."[5]

Psychology talks about attitudinal health. Those who study the mind and mental processes are aware of how important an attitude is. We need to know that a right attitude is vital to our walk in the Spirit.

I like the story of the little crippled boy who was asked one time how he could face the future and be involved with living when he was so crippled. The boy's reply was, "It never touched my heart." We need to make

14

sure that our faulty concepts, our disappointments in people, our failures, never touch our hearts. For when we come to a study of the Spirit-filled life we must be open to God's work in our lives. An attitude of disbelief or doubt will be a barrier to progress.

Summary

OBJECTIVE: TO BE HOLY.

Keep these scriptures marked in your Bible for reference and study. Better yet, memorize them!

- Ephesians 1:4
    - Romans 12:1
        - Colossians 1:22
            - Colossians 3:12
                - 1 Peter 1:15-16

A Positive Thought

God's will for you is to be holy—to live a holy life. You cannot do this without His help. He will help you at all times. That is His promise! You must believe, trust His Word, and follow the steps He shows you. You must be open and obedient. Open yourself to the journey with God and to a holy life!

JESUS CALLS US

Jesus calls us; o'er the tumult
Of our life's wild, restless sea,
Day by day His sweet voice soundeth,
Saying, "Christian, follow Me."

Jesus calls us from the worship
Of the vain world's golden store,

15

From each idol that would keep us,
*   Saying, "Christian, love Me more."*

In our joys and in our sorrows,
*   Days of toil and hours of ease,*
Still He calls, in cares and pleasures,
*   "Christian, love Me more than these."*

Jesus calls us. By Thy mercies,
*   Saviour, may we hear Thy call,*
Give our hearts to Thy obedience,
*   Serve and love Thee best of all.*

                    —Cecil F. Alexander

Chapter 2

The Goal of the
Spirit-filled Life

God's goal for us is holiness, and the goal for the Spirit-filled life is to fulfill this plan, moving along a day at a time, getting to know Christ better.

A goal is a "step" on the road to the objective – something that can be done to bring the objective into reality. Someone has said that "a goal is a statement about what we hope to do or be tomorrow, or next week, or next year." A goal should be measurable and accomplishable. Edward R. Dayton says that "the Christian's goals are faith's response to God's imperative, and thus reflect an additional dimension, our part in God's plan."[1] God has made possible the holy life for the Christian. But the Christian must apply himself, daily, in such ways that will allow God access to his heart.

Milo L. Arnold tells of a boyhood friend who had lofty ideas, but never put any work into them. Arnold said, "He thought tomorrow could explode full-grown without depending upon yesterday for preparation."[2] The objective, "to be holy," will not suddenly just happen. It is the result of daily responses to the Holy Spirit. And if one does not have the objective identified through goals –

walking in the Spirit, daily—then the objective will elude him.

General Motors reached its objective by periodic goal-setting, then putting its energies to the accomplishment of those goals. As the goals were accomplished, one by one, there unfolded the giant industry. I am not suggesting that the sanctified life is so automatic as to come about by simply listing and accomplishing goals. I am suggesting, however, that unless one has in mind where he wants to go in his spiritual walk, he may be prone to detours and distractions. Goals, if for no other reason, keep the spiritual desires from being sidetracked.

Terry Muck gives us this good caution on goals: "The danger of goals, of course, is that they fit us with blinders in our intentness to achieve them. In proper perspective, goals can point us in the right direction; however, legalistically sought, goals can put us in a rut so deep we fail to see God's guiding hand waving at us to change direction."[3]

The Bible encourages us along the line of goal-setting. *The Living Bible* paraphrases 2 Corinthians 10:13 to read, "Our goal is to measure up to God's plan for us." Note the phrase, "God's plan for us." That's important! We need to keep in mind that our goal must be God-oriented, not people-oriented, or even church-oriented.

One major hindrance on the journey to the Spirit-filled life is people. Listening to too many opinions can be confusing. Some people's comments leave you sidetracked and disappointed. They do not mean to give you confusing signals and advice. But they give you instructions from their own background and walk with God. It may be relevant, or it may not be. If they are ahead of you in their walk with God, they may be putting too much stretch in your walk, while others may be beginners themselves, and lead you astray because they are not certain of teachings themselves.

Stay close to the Bible. Study it, daily. Check out the advice your friends give you—yes, even the preacher's word. Be sure what is said can be backed up by biblical principles, and ask people to show you where the principle is found in the Bible. If it isn't there, discard what is said and go with the Word. Keep life aligned with the Word and you'll come out where God wants you.

If our objective is to be holy, then the goal of our spiritual life must be to know Christ better. It is helpful to keep in mind that God expects growth only a day at a time. He does not expect us to achieve our objective in one giant spiritual step. Maturity and adulthood come, but we must crawl before walking and childhood precedes adolescence and adulthood. Our God is understanding of our day-to-day journey.

Consider these scriptures. Study them to get an idea of your goal for the spiritual journey:

Matthew 22:37	1 Peter 1:2
Hebrews 10:22	2 Peter 1:5
2 Corinthians 7:1	2 Peter 3:18

The goal in our spiritual journey is important. It helps us to measure progress, not by what others say should be happening, but by what *we know* is happening. God is not comparing your walk with Him with that of any other. He is uniquely interested in *your* progress. He wants you to make it! He wants you to grow and have a victorious life all of your own. So, your goal is personal—move *your* life, one day or step at a time, toward God.

God does not say, "Now compared with Christian A, you are a little behind schedule." Never! He says, "According to your ability, and from where you're coming, and taking into consideration what you are working through, you are on target! Keep growing!"

Summary

GOAL: To move life, a day at a time,
toward the fulfillment of God's plan.

Here are some scriptures to study:
- Philippians 1:6
  - Philippians 3:14
    - Colossians 2:6
      - 1 Peter 1:2
        - Matthew 22:37
          - Hebrews 10:22
            - 2 Corinthians 7:1
              - 2 Peter 1:5
                - 2 Peter 3:18

A Positive Thought

God is helping you grow into a spiritually mature person, day by day, as you keep your heart open to Him through obedience. He does not compare you with others. He nurtures you in a personal, loving way. Believe you are making progress. Do not be discouraged. The fashioning process takes time, but stay on the journey!

A CHARGE TO KEEP I HAVE

A charge to keep I have,
A God to glorify;
A never-dying soul to save,
And fit it for the sky.

To serve the present age,
*   My calling to fulfill;*
Oh, may it all my pow'rs engage
*   To do my Master's will!*

Arm me with jealous care,
*   As in Thy sight to live;*
And, oh, Thy servant, Lord, prepare
*   A strict account to give!*

Help me to watch and pray,
*   And on thyself rely,*
Assured if I my trust betray
*   I shall forever die.*

—Charles Wesley

Chapter 3

The Plan – the First Step

The greatest objective or goal will fail without a plan. While it is good to have a stated objective and a written, well-defined goal, without a plan it only remains a thought in the mind or a dream on paper. Every pursuit of a goal has a vital first step.

For each of us the "check-in" point for the journey to the sanctified life will vary. We will come from different levels of understanding and maturity. Some will come from church backgrounds, while others will be coming to the faith with little or no knowledge.

Do not despair if you come to the Christian journey with little or no background or knowledge. God does not have levels of grace and blessing for those more learned in the ways of faith. His commands and His ways are the same for all. So, do not hesitate to step out on the pathway. His plan is unique for you and you can claim all His benefits through obedience and trust. Remember some thoughts from Chapter 2. God does not compare you with others. He takes you where you are and nurtures you in love and grace.

Your First Step

The first step for all who set out in pursuit of the objective "to be holy" is conversion. Conversion is also known as the new birth, being born again, or being saved. These terms have the same basic meaning: transformation. The "plan" for accomplishing this step is *repentance*. Repentance is an admonition of the New Testament. Here are some scriptures for you to study:

> Mark 1:14-15 – "Jesus went into Galilee, proclaiming the good news of God. 'The time has come,' he said. 'The kingdom of God is near. Repent and believe the good news!' "

> Mark 6:12 – "They went out and preached that people should repent."

> Luke 13:1-3 – "Now there were some present at that time who told Jesus about the Galileans whose blood Pilate had mixed with their sacrifices. Jesus answered, 'Do you think that these Galileans were worse sinners than all the other Galileans because they suffered this way? I tell you, no! But unless you repent, you too will all perish.' "

> Acts 2:38 – "Peter replied, 'Repent and be baptized, every one of you, in the name of Jesus Christ so that your sins may be forgiven.' "

> Acts 3:19 – "Repent, then, and turn to God, so that your sins may be wiped out, that times of refreshing may come from the Lord."

Repentance has been defined as "godly sorrow for sin." It is a decision to turn from sin and go with God. It is a determination to forsake sin and actively seek righteousness. Second Corinthians 7:10 states, "Godly sorrow brings repentance that leads to salvation."

John Seamands reminds us that *repentance* "connotes a profound transformation involving a change of mind, will, and heart." He mentions that in the Kekchi language [of Guatemala], it is translated "it pains my heart." In Baouli, West Africa, the same concept is expressed as "It hurts so much I want to quit."[1]

The first factor you face in repentance is coming to grips with sin. A sin has been defined as a "wilful transgression of a known law of God." The journey to the new birth, then encounters a clash of wills—the will of sin, described in Romans 7, that seeks its own, and the will of God that requires forsaking of the evil ways.

At first you might think it easy to break the sinful habits. But you will experience just the opposite. Your first attempts to be free from sin will only reveal its bondage. Picture a dog chained to a stake. He is fast asleep, not aware that he has been chained. He awakens, nibbles at the food near his kennel, still unmindful of the chain. But suppose you move the food just beyond the reach of the chain. The dog, not aware of his bondage, rushes toward the food. Just before he reaches it, he feels the restraint. His efforts to reach the food are in vain. For the first time, he feels the bondage!

This is a picture of sin. We are not aware of sin's grasp until we seek freedom. Then the awakening and realization come.

There is only one way to deal with sin. That is to confess it and forsake it. Repentance is the expression of the heart that confesses its sinfulness and affirms its decision to seek the ways of God. Repentance is my confessing the brokenness of my life because of sin, and laying that brokenness at the foot of the Cross. Vance Havner says, "God uses broken things. It takes broken soil to produce a crop, broken clouds to give rain, broken grain to give bread, broken bread to give strength. When we are broken, because of sin, and acknowledge this before Christ, we open the door to healing, through conversion and the new birth."[2]

There are three steps in the conversion experience:

1. **Realize** that you are a sinner. Romans 3:23 states that "all have sinned and fall short of the glory of God."

2. **Repent.** Confess your sins and turn from them. First John 1:9 tells us: "If we confess our sins, he is faithful and just and will forgive us our sin."

3. **Receive** Christ into your heart through faith. Revelation 3:20 says: "Here I am! I stand at the door and knock. If anyone hears my voice and opens the door, I will come in and eat with him, and he with me."

What Happens Then?

What happens when a sinner repents and receives Christ into his heart? Four things happen simultaneously. It is important to grasp these before we move on in the journey to the Spirit-filled life. They are:

1. **Regeneration.** One is "born again." Spiritual life begins. The "new birth" occurs as God gives spiritual life to a heart/spirit that was "dead in trespasses and sins." The *Manual of the Church of the Nazarene* states this about regeneration: "We believe that regeneration, or the new birth, is that gracious work of God whereby the moral nature of the repentant believer is spiritually quickened and given a distinctively spiritual life, capable of faith, love, and obedience" (par. 10).

2. **Justification.** In the mind of God, the believer is considered "free from the acts of sin." God, through justification, lifts the penalty of his sins and they are no longer credited against him. The *Manual* states: "We believe that justification is the gracious and judicial act of God by which He grants full pardon of all guilt and complete release from the penalty of sins committed, and acceptance as righteous, to all who believe on Jesus Christ and receive Him as Lord and Saviour" (par. 9).

3. **Forgiveness.** Our sins and our sinful acts have been forgiven, and the guilt they incurred is removed. It means that we stand before God with a "blameless" record, as everything charged against us has been erased, forgiven.

4. **Adoption.** We are brought into the family of God. We are adopted into the family as "children of God." Study Romans 8 and Colossians 1:13-14. The *Manual* has this paragraph on adoption: "We believe that adoption is that gracious act of God by which the justified and regenerated believer is constituted a son of God" (par. 11).

Every man enters his pilgrimage to the Spirit-filled life through repentance. This "born-again" experience is the threshold into new life in Christ. After this, growth in Christ is the plan. That unfolds in a variety of exercises, which will be discussed in Chapter 4.

Summary

PLAN: The procedures to be followed to accomplish the goal of attaining the Spirit-filled life.

The starting point is our repentance followed by God's forgiveness and our becoming thereby a part of the family of God. We are now on the way to the goal of the holy life.

Scriptures to study:
- Mark 1:14-15
  - Mark 6:12
    - Luke 13:1-3
      - Acts 2:38
        - Acts 3:19
          - 2 Corinthians 7:10
- Romans 7
  - Romans 8

- Romans 3:23
    - 1 John 1:9
        - Revelation 3:20
            - Romans 10:9-10
                - Colossians 1:13-15

A Positive Thought

God gives you instructions in His Word. As you follow them obediently, you grow and understand. If you stay with His plan, you can be confident of victory. And the first step in His plan is repentance.

JESUS, I COME

Out of my bondage, sorrow, and night,
Jesus, I come; Jesus, I come,
Into Thy freedom, gladness, and light,
Jesus, I come to Thee.
Out of my sickness into Thy health,
Out of my want and into Thy wealth,
Out of my sin and into thyself,
Jesus, I come to Thee.

Out of my shameful failure and loss,
Jesus, I come; Jesus, I come,
Into the glorious gain of Thy cross,
Jesus, I come to Thee.
Out of earth's sorrows into Thy balm,
Out of life's storms and into Thy calm,
Out of distress to jubilant psalm,
Jesus, I come to Thee.

Out of unrest and arrogant pride,
Jesus, I come; Jesus, I come,

Into Thy blessed will to abide,
Jesus, I come to Thee.
Out of myself to dwell in Thy love,
Out of despair into raptures above,
Upward for aye on wings like a dove,
Jesus, I come to Thee.

Out of the fear and dread of the tomb,
Jesus, I come; Jesus, I come,
Into the joy and light of Thy home,
Jesus, I come to Thee.
Out of the depths of ruin untold,
Into the peace of Thy sheltering fold,
Ever Thy glorious face to behold,
Jesus, I come to Thee.

—W. T. SLEEPER

Chapter 4

Organization –
the Disciplines of Life

Organization answers the "How do I get there?" question. Organization is concerned with growth. Organization is the process for moving into the arena of action in our pilgrimage with God. Growth is the key factor here.

G – GOD'S
R – REGENERATION
O – OPENING
W – WINDOWS
T – TO
H – (THE) HEART

Just as the body grows through daily exercise and nourishment, the Christian grows through daily exercise and nourishment. Some of the ways Christians grow will be discussed in this chapter. They are the disciplines around which life needs to be organized, to insure growth and learning.

Prayer

Prayer is the number one discipline. Prayer is the breathing of the soul – the talking and listening to God that is so vital. Prayer is the channel of communication between man and God.

Pauline Spray, in her book *Coping with Tension*, observes that "Prayer puts us in touch with God's love."[1] Another has observed that before we can make much progress along the spiritual path, we must find handles to the deep emotions of life. Prayer is one discipline that helps.

Adam Clarke advised: "Pray much in private. Without this you will find it utterly impossible to keep yourself in the love of God."[2]

Here are some scriptures that encourage prayer:

Psalm 32:6

Matthew 5:44

Matthew 6:5-13

Matthew 26:41

Mark 14:38

Luke 6:28

Luke 11:1-4

Luke 18:1

Luke 21:36

1 Thessalonians 5:17

Hebrews 13:19

James 5:13-16

1 Peter 4:7

Bible Study

Bible study is another important discipline. The emphasis should be on study. While it is good to read the Bible, it is necessary also to *study* the Bible. Use a good commentary, like *Beacon Bible Commentary*, available from the Nazarene Publishing House.

The Christian grows through what he learns from the Word. As the heart and mind are exposed to the truth the Christian responds, thus allowing life to change and move toward the ways of God.

Some time ago *Leadership* magazine polled its readers concerning their devotional lives, and in particular, they asked about Bible study. One said, "Regular

Bible reading gives me a standard against which I can measure myself. Prayer awakens my longing for God; Bible study gives me a map for living."[3]

Here are some scriptures that encourage Bible study:
> Psalm 119:9-16
> > Psalm 119:105
> > > 2 Timothy 2:15
> > > > James 1:5-6

Worship

Worship is a vital discipline for the Christian. Worship means bringing the heart and mind into reverence before God—to praise Him, learn from Him, adore Him, listen to Him. It gives opportunity for the soul to stand at attention before God and give allegiance to His Word and His ways.

Dr. Keith W. Sehnert, in his book *Stress/Unstress* says: "Each act of worship, prayer, and meditation adds to the fabric of spiritual life like individual fibers in a tapestry."[4]

Here are some scriptures that encourage worship:

Psalm 92:2	Luke 4:8
Psalm 95:6	John 4:20-24
Psalm 96:9	Acts 24:14
Psalm 99:5, 9	Romans 12:1
Psalm 132:7	Hebrews 10:19

Stewardship and Giving

Giving is also an important discipline. One characteristic you see in God is giving, and its greatest expression was the giving of His only begotten Son for our salvation. Giving is God's method for molding hearts. Through giving we express our priorities, our love, our concern.

The Christian should learn early in his walk with God that giving is an expression of love. Where it is cultivated it expands the heart to receive God's blessing. Where it is restrained, it pulls the cords of selfishness around the heart.

Some scriptures that encourage giving are:
Malachi 3:8-12
Luke 6:38
2 Corinthians 9:7

Fellowship

Fellowship is a joyful experience for the Christian, but it is also a discipline. The Christian not only needs the fellowship of other Christians, but he also needs to share his life with others.

Here are some scriptures that encourage fellowship:

Acts 2:42-47	Galatians 2:9
Acts 20:7	Hebrews 10:25
1 Corinthians 1:9	1 John 1:3, 7

Witnessing

Witnessing is a vital discipline for the Christian. Someone has described witnessing as simply "one beggar telling another beggar where to find bread." We once were beggars; now we are God's children, with plenty to share! Too many times we are frightened off from witnessing because we feel we must be a professional at it. Our most valuable witnessing is our telling in simple testimony the experience of our pilgrimage with Jesus.

Some scriptures that encourage witnessing are:
Isaiah 43:10-12
Isaiah 44:8
Acts 1:8

Serving

Service is a necessary discipline. Through serving God, the church, and others, the Christian builds bridges over which the Spirit can nurture and build. Someone wrote, "By the pathway of duty flows the river of God's grace."

Here are some scriptures that encourage service:

Psalm 100:2   Ephesians 4:7-13
Matthew 4:10   Ephesians 6:7
Romans 12:1-2   Hebrews 9:14
Galatians 5:13

The Christian goal is continued growth in spiritual life. But it will not happen unless our lives are disciplined and organized around the priorities of Christian living. By attending to the priorities well, we open life to the nurture of God.

A successful business must function within its organizational structure. Chaos and disorder occur if this is ignored. If the Christian seeking the benefits of the Spirit-filled life ignores the necessary disciplines, eventually growth is stagnated and backsliding can occur.

Summary

ORGANIZATION: The necessary methods/ingredients/ disciplines that insure growth and attainment of the goals for the Spirit-filled life.

Go back over the scriptures in this chapter. Focus on some of them for study and memorization.

A Positive Thought

Christian growth progresses best when disciplines are properly exercised and priorities are honored. Organize and discipline your life in ways that will allow spiritual growth. The journey with God will then be exciting!

TAKE MY LIFE, AND LET IT BE

Take my life, and let it be
Consecrated, Lord, to Thee.
Take my hands and let them move
At the impulse of Thy love,
At the impulse of Thy love.

Take my feet, and let them be
Swift and beautiful for Thee.
Take my voice, and let me sing
Always, only, for my King;
Always, only, for my King.

Take my lips, and let them be
Filled with messages for Thee.
Take my silver and my gold;
Not a mite would I withhold,
Not a mite would I withhold.

Take my will and make it Thine;
It shall be no longer mine.
Take my heart; it is Thine own!
It shall be Thy royal throne.
It shall be Thy royal throne.

Take my love; my God, I pour
At Thy feet its treasure store.
Take myself and I will be
Ever, only, all for Thee;
Ever, only, all for Thee.

—FRANCES R. HAVERGAL

Chapter 5

Implementation — Moving on to Entire Sanctification

In the implementation stage of our pilgrimage, we are concerned with doing. Most would agree that it is not more knowledge that we need. All of us know more now than we are using. Our need is to simply act on the knowledge we have. As we put into action what we discussed in the previous chapter, we gain spiritual strength and become more like Christ.

But as we journey we become increasingly aware of an inhibiting force within — the sin nature so vividly described in Romans 7. Like Paul we cry out for deliverance. How can we fully live the holy life God expects of us as long as we have to struggle against the inherited sin within the heart?

Just as God provided the remedy for sins committed through forgiveness, so He provided the remedy for the sin nature through cleansing. And just as repentance is the avenue to forgiveness, so consecration is the avenue to cleansing — to entire sanctification. Consecration is our yielding the last bastion of our wills to God.

The term *yield* defines well what consecration is, for here is implied a willingness on our part to turn everything we have and are over to God. To yield is to say yes to God and to give full allegiance to His commands. To yield is to acknowledge Jesus as Lord of our lives and to submit to that Lordship.

If we are to grow in the sanctified life, we must yield to the Spirit's ways and the Spirit's Word. We must surrender our desires. We must submit to the Lordship of Christ. E. Stanley Jones reminds us that "all life is lifted by surrender to something higher. The mineral to the plant; the plant to the animal; the animal to man; and man to God."[1]

Consecration is man's part in the sanctifying process. God, through His Spirit, sanctifies that which is separated for His use. Consecration is our separating ourselves—by our choice and an act of our will, through faith—to God. God then responds with cleansing, empowerment, and sanctification.

But it is important for us to understand the growth process between salvation and entire sanctification. When we are saved, converted, born again, we enter into a relationship with Christ. While it is a relationship of new life and forgiveness, it is also a learning relationship. We are learning something about ourselves, something about God, and something about sin. It is not necessarily the time involved in the process that is important, but the quality of that spiritual deepening.

Repentance deals with sins committed for which we are responsible and for which we seek divine forgiveness. Consecration deals with the giving of our redeemed selves to God for His complete control. Repentance is something a *sinner* does, while consecration is the privilege of the *believer*. Repentance leads to freedom from sin's past, while consecration leads to freedom from sin's pull.

The growing process from repentance to consecration is a kind of continuation of the conversion experience. At repentance a person is changed, regenerated, justified, forgiven, and adopted into the family of God. He is converted from sinfulness to righteousness. But the conversion that began at repentance is a process that must continue through growth and continued learning. For, in obedience to my resolve at the time of being saved to "walk in the light," that light is changing me:

> from darkness to light,
> from death to life,
> from self-ways to Christ's ways,
> from flesh-ways to the Spirit's ways,
> from slavery to freedom,
> from guilt to forgiveness,
> from despair to hope,
> from sinfulness to righteousness.

Second Corinthians 5:17 assures us that "if anyone is in Christ, he is a new creation; the old has gone, the new has come!" While there is a moment in time, which we call the crisis of conversion, when we are changed and brought into new life and a redemptive relationship with Christ, there remains the learning, growing, changing process that acclimates us to the converted state. Could we, without injustice to the Scriptures, say that though the old has gone (and in our minds and life it is still going), the new has come (and in our total selves, it is still coming).

The process of moving from repentance to consecration means that as we walk with Christ daily — praying, studying the Word, thinking about Him — we get to know Him better, to know ourselves better, and to understand sin and righteousness in a more perceptive way. Hence,

> my appetites,
> my desires,
> my will,

> my selfishness,
> my finances,
> my relationships,
> my priorities,
> my marriage,
> my free time,
> my job . . .

are all being elevated to GOD-CONSCIOUS levels.

From repentance to consecration we are in the "converting process" of becoming more like Christ wants us to become. Romans 12:2 admonishes, "Do not conform any longer to the pattern of this world, but be transformed by the renewing of your mind. Then you will be able to test and approve what God's will is—his good, pleasing and perfect will." This is the essence of spiritual growth, or what we may think of as the "converting process." From the moment we accept Christ, we begin the journey of learning His perfect will for our lives.

But we cannot grow in relationship with Christ without becoming conscious of sin's pull and power. As we become more God-conscious, we become deeply aware of sin's poison in our spiritual system. Paul put it this way in Romans 7:21-23: "I find this law at work: When I want to do good, evil is right there with me. For in my inner being I delight in God's law; but I see another law at work in the members of my body, waging war against the law of my mind and making me a prisoner of the law of sin at work within my members."

The Christian in process, then, must deal with sin, radically and resolutely, because during this process of growth after we are saved, we become aware that sin is threatening our relationship with Christ. We see sin, now, as that which destroys spiritual life and hinders our spiritual quest. Such a consciousness of sin within brings us to the place of seeking deliverance, which comes through consecration: yielding our total self to God for the Spirit's cleansing and the dethronement of sin. And when we yield our all, the Spirit sanctifies.

Hannah Whitall Smith, in her classic, *The Christian's Secret of a Happy Life*, writes:

> Oh, be generous in your self-surrender! Meet His measureless devotion for you with a measureless devotion to Him. Be glad and eager to throw yourself unreservedly into His loving arms, and to hand over the reins of government to Him. Whatever there is of you, let Him have it all. Give up forever everything that is separate from Him. Consent to resign, from this time forward, all liberty of choice and glory in the blessed nearness of union.[2]

The simple steps of consecration are these:

1. **Acknowledge** the presence of sin in the heart (Romans 7). Admit that it is bigger than you and that you cannot deal with it apart from the Spirit's help.

2. **Ask** for God's help by yielding right-of-way to His Spirit (Romans 12:1-2).

3. **Accept,** by faith, His sanctification! He who promises to make you holy, will, by His power and by the blood of the Atonement, cleanse and remove the rudiments of sin (1 Thessalonians 5:23-24).

Summary

IMPLEMENTATION: Moving life from the knowledge of the Spirit's way to the *doing* of what the Spirit teaches. Implementation brings one to the yielded life, consecration, where the Spirit sanctifies.

Here are some scriptures you will want to refer to:

- 2 Corinthians 5:17
- Romans 12:1-2
- Colossians 2:6-7
- Romans 7:21-23
- 1 Thessalonians 5:23-24

A Positive Thought

God has promised victory for each of His children. When we say a final yes to the will of God, and a firm no to the things of the world, we can lay claim to God's promised cleansing, through faith. God has called us to holiness, and He will meet our needs!

O to Be Like Thee

Oh, to be like Thee! blessed Redeemer,
This is my constant longing and prayer.
Gladly I'll forfeit all of earth's treasures,
Jesus, Thy perfect likeness to wear.

Oh, to be like Thee! full of compassion,
Loving, forgiving, tender and kind,
Helping the helpless, cheering the fainting,
Seeking the wand'ring sinner to find!

Oh, to be like Thee! lowly in spirit,
Holy and harmless, patient and brave;
Meekly enduring cruel reproaches,
Willing to suffer others to save.

Oh, to be like Thee! Lord, I am coming,
Now to receive th' anointing divine.
All that I am and have I am bringing;
Lord, from this moment all shall be Thine.

40

Oh, to be like Thee! While I am pleading,
Pour out Thy Spirit, fill with Thy love;
Make me a temple meet for Thy dwelling,
Fit me for life and heaven above.

Oh, to be like Thee! Oh, to be like Thee,
Blessed Redeemer, pure as Thou art!
Come in Thy sweetness, come in Thy fullness;
Stamp Thine own image deep on my heart.

—T. O. CHISHOLM

Chapter 6

Control – Living Under
the Lordship of Christ

Control is the "walking in the Spirit" part of the sanctified life. After consecration, where the heart/spirit has said yes to the will of God and the Holy Spirit has responded with cleansing and sanctification, the spiritual pilgrimage continues on a heightened level. The battle within is over. Sin has been cleansed from the heart. The continued filling of the Spirit strengthens the inner man.

When we talk about "control" we are talking about a consecration that has yielded the inner territory of the heart/spirit to the Holy Spirit. Jesus, then, reigns as "commander in chief." Jesus is Lord!

Before consecration the heart/spirit was subject to the sinful nature and its dominance. At conversion, the acts of sin are forgiven, but the pollution of sin remains. Consecration brings to life cleansing from the pollution of sin. So, what was filled with sin is now filled with God. For in yielding to the Spirit of God, one's heart/spirit has invited God to enter – to enter totally – to fill and to cleanse every part. Such a total yieldedness invites Christ to sit on the throne of life as Savior and as Sanctifier.

Jesus, as Lord of life, directs the activities of the heart in the sanctified life and determines the atmosphere of the heart. Paul's admonition in Ephesians 5:18, "Be filled with the Spirit," is a summons to every believer to allow the Spirit to fill—and to keep on filling (as we keep on yielding).

The heart/spirit of man is going to be filled with something—or Someone! Either darkness or light, evil or good, death or life, self or God, sin or righteousness. When we yield to the Spirit, the filling is of God and life is then filled with the good things of God.

The first thing we need to remember in the experience of sanctification is that life must be under the control of the Spirit. Let's think about some way this can be accomplished.

1. *Plant your life in the Word of God.* Put all your spiritual roots down into God's Word. Study and meditate upon its truth and acquaint yourself with its message to you.

2. *Bring life—all of life—under the authority of the Word of God.* Consider these scriptures: 1 Peter 1:2, 5; 2 Peter 3:18; Psalm 119:12, 18; 2 Timothy 2:15.

In consecration we turn over every part of life to the ways of God. The point of struggle is no longer one between self and God. We have yielded the right of way to Jesus, and the heart/spirit must be kept under His control.

Oswald Chambers writes:

> The characteristic of a man who begins to walk in the light is that he drags himself into the light all the time. He does not make excuses for things done in the dark; he brings everything to the light, and says, "This is to be condemned; this does not belong to Jesus Christ," and so keeps in the light.[1]

3. *Abide in Christ.* Study John 15 and Colossians 2:6-7. The yielded life is life centered in Christ, letting

Jesus be Lord. To be Lord means He must rule and reign at all times.

Charlie W. Shedd makes this interesting point: "Jesus has no limits. Whenever I give Him free play in my soul, He increases its capacity. He stretches out the heart for more of Himself."[2]

4. *Commit life to the right.* Psalm 119:11 says, "I have hidden your word in my heart that I might not sin against you." To be committed to the Word is to be committed to the right. It is not a question of the right being convenient or comfortable. The sanctified life does not provide such an option. Where Jesus is Lord there is only the right way.

5. *Build obedience into your life.* Psalm 25:10 reads "All the ways of the Lord are loving and faithful for those who keep the demands of his covenant." Obedience is always right. Disobedience gives the enemy opportunity to dethrone Jesus as Lord, to sidetrack our sanctified life.

6. *Learn to trust.* Study Proverbs 3:5-6. Someone has said that "the call of God will not take you where the grace of God will not keep you." This is true in the call to holy living. God would not call us to a state of grace and then not provide the power to keep us along the journey. He *will* keep us; it is ours simply to trust our daily lives to His Lordship and His care.

7. *Practice the privilege of prayer.* Huber L. Drumwright has said, "Habits will hinder our prayer life, or prayer will reform our habits."[3] Living the sanctified life is a matter of constant yielding at the point of our choices. When something that becomes a struggle or a temptation enters the life there is a way out. That way is through prayer. It is too often the route least traveled. Study 1 Corinthians 10:13.

8. *Exercise faith.* Learning to trust will determine to a large degree your peace with God. Faith grows only as

44

it is exercised. The more of life you commit to God, in faith, the more you will see what God can do. Paul's admonition is, "The life I live in the body, I live by faith in the Son of God" (Galatians 2:20).

Rufus Jones has said, "Let a person's inner being be fortified with a faith in God, and all his creative powers are heightened, and his grip on everyday things is immensely increased. It is as though he has tapped a hidden reservoir of power."[4]

Summary

CONTROL: Yielding life to the Spirit, keeping life under the authority of Jesus, acknowledging Him as Lord of life.

Keep these scriptures before you:

- 1 Peter 1:2, 5
  - 2 Peter 3:18
    - Psalm 119:12, 18
      - 2 Timothy 2:15
        - John 15
- Colossians 2:6-7
  - Psalm 119:11
    - Proverbs 3:5-6
      - 1 Corinthians 10:13
        - Galatians 2:20

A Positive Thought

God's promise is to keep that which is committed to Him. He is a God of victory. He wills peace and victory for each of His children. Our part in spiritual victory is yielding our all to Him and obeying His will for our lives.

Have Thine Own Way, Lord

Have Thine own way, Lord! Have Thine own way!
Thou art the Potter; I am the clay.
Mold me and make me after Thy will,
While I am waiting, yielded and still.

Have Thine own way, Lord! Have Thine own way!
Search me and try me, Master, today!
Whiter than snow, Lord, wash me just now,
As in Thy presence humbly I bow.

Have Thine own way, Lord! Have Thine own way!
Wounded and weary, help me, I pray!
Power—all power—surely is Thine!
Touch me and heal me, Saviour divine!

Have Thine own way, Lord! Have Thine own way!
Hold o'er my being absolute sway!
Fill with Thy Spirit till all shall see
Christ only, always living in me![5]

—ADELAINE A. POLLARD

Chapter 7

Concepts of God

Probably nothing has hindered us more in understanding the spiritual life and enjoying its benefits than an inadequate concept of God. A limited conception of Him will prevent our comprehending the full meaning of the grace of God and will keep us from reaching out for all the benefits of the grace of God. E. Stanley Jones says our view of God needs cleansing.

A. W. Tozer put some helpful thoughts about God in his book *The Knowledge of the Holy*. He wrote:

> What comes into our minds when we think about God is the most important thing about us. The most portentous fact about any man is not what he at a given time may say or do, but what he in his deep heart conceived God to be like. We tend by a secret law of the soul to move toward our mental image of God.
>
> Were we able to extract from any man a complete answer to the question, "What comes into your mind when you think about God?" we might predict with certainty the spiritual future of that man.[1]

The following diagrams may help us see some of the faulty concepts of God that hinder our spiritual growth.

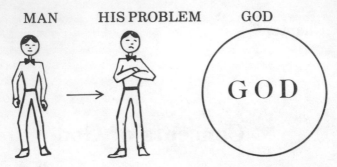

MAN HIS PROBLEM GOD

GOD

In this diagram man's problem with God is himself. He sees everything, in relation to God, through self. The self that he often sees is sinful and unworthy of God's love and goodness. He fails to add the dimension of grace and mercy to the picture, so his half-finished concept of God is a deterrent to growth and trust.

In his book *The Guilt Trip* Hal Lindsey mentions how failures affect our relationship with God:

Because we're always aware that in many ways we fall short of what we should be as Christians, it's only natural to assume that God must be displeased with our performance. The more we let God down, the more we assume His anger, until such alienation sets into our minds that it is virtually impossible for us to enjoy a vital fellowship with God.[2]

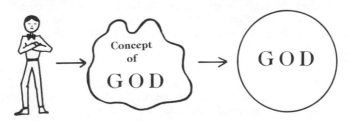

In this diagram man has a warped concept of God. He sees God as the stern law-giver, harsh, wrathful, waiting to catch man in a sin or mistake so He can render punishment. Fear is the undertone of this idea. It keeps love, forgiveness, mercy, and grace from filtering through. Such a concept makes it hard for man to accept the offered forgiveness of God.

John T. Seamands reminds us that "God is not against us because of our sin, but is for us against our sin."[3] We need to fix this in our mind so we can approach a God who wills victory for us.

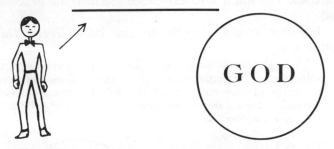

In this diagram man has a transcendent, exalted view of God. He cannot comprehend God being bothered with man's problems. With such a view, a personal relationship between God and man is out of the question. This concept views God as Someone who is moved to action only in the tragic epochs of history, but never as a God who is interested in the day-to-day activities of man.

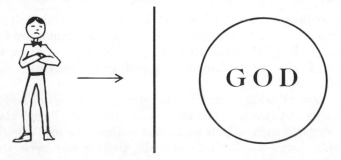

In this view of God, one's concept has been carved out of life's adverse experiences. And all the experiences have been charged against God. A tragic death, an unanswered prayer, fears, and failures are all charged against the love of God—failure on God's part to "do something." Loss and disappointment pile up until there is a wall of resistance against God. As every spiritual possibility or experience is filtered through this view, the heart and the mind are barricaded against the grace of God.

Hannah Whitall Smith, in her book *Every Day Religion,* says:

> We take the worst elements in our own characters, our selfishness, our impatience, our suspiciousness, our hard thoughts of one another, as the key to interpret God, instead of taking our best elements, of love, and self-sacrifice, and patience, as the key.[4]

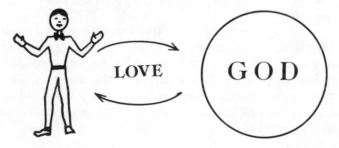

A proper way to view God is to see Him and understand Him as a God of love. John's emphatic summary is "God is love" (1 John 4:16). The Cross is proof of how much God loves us. This is wrapped up so beautifully in John 3:16.

When God is seen, first, as relating to us out of love, it helps us to understand all that He does and all that He is. For instance, a God who loves with *agape* love—self-giving love—would hate the sin that would seek to destroy His children. This wrath-side of God can be better understood when we realize that it is coming from a heart of love. And because He loves, He must act.

There is one more diagram needed to make the picture complete.

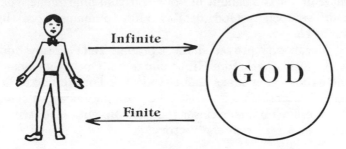

God must be seen as an infinite Being. Thus, He is not limited in knowledge, in wisdom, in resources, in grace, in mercy, in love—in all that is so uniquely God.

But man is finite. At his wisest he is limited in knowledge. At his best he is earthbound and limited because of humanness.

What this concept allows is that the things that stagger the mind of man are pure thoughts with God. The sorrows and tragedies that prompt man's "why?" find their ultimate answers in the infinite God who sees the total dimension of life. He, then, being infinite, can take the worst and weave out of it something of beauty and meaning. That man cannot do.

Conclusion

It is easy to see from the various possible concepts of God how easy it would be to cast God in a wrong mold and miss the benefits of relationship and trust. Often it is necessary for us to "unlearn" some things we have been taught and to reprogram our thinking. And this is probably more true about out concepts of God than of any other area of our spiritual lives.

Such mental and emotional pursuits are not easy. It is difficult to change a pattern that has been years forming. But for the benefit of your spiritual pilgrimage, you must be open to God to allow Him to change you. He wants to.

Begin with prayer—honest prayer. Tell God how you really feel. Lay before Him your fears. Open your heart and expose your ideas about God. Ask Him to make the needed alterations. Be assured of His patience and help. Then, move on into a closer relationship with God, trusting Him for growth and victory!

Chapter 8

What If . . . ?

"What if I sin after I am sanctified?" That's a good question. Most of us ask it at one time or another. Let's get a scriptural perspective, first.

First John 2:1-2 says: "But if anybody does sin, we have one who speaks to the Father in our defense—Jesus Christ, the Righteous One. He is the atoning sacrifice for our sins, and not only for ours but also for the sins of the whole world." We need to build our foundation of repentance on this very thought, that if we do sin, we have One to whom we can go, and that is Jesus Christ. This is the promise that sometimes gets lost in the aftermath of sin.

Now, because the sanctified life is one lived in obedience to God, where the heart wills only the will of God, we should not have much of a problem with sin. As 1 John 1:7 assures us, "If we walk in the light, as he is in the light, we have fellowship with one another, and the blood of Jesus, his Son, purifies us from all sin."

The important thing for us to remember is that if we keep the love of the Father nurtured in our hearts through fellowship, trust, obedience, and prayer, sin will not enter our life. This very love relationship with God is a deterrent to sin. Someone gave good advice when he said, "Prepare and prevent rather than repair and repent."

What happens, however, when the love wanes and in

an unguarded moment the heart transgresses? One of two things can happen. We can feel utter failure in our spiritual walk and give up. Unfortunately, many do this. Sin brings a sense of failure, which can be so overwhelming that its very sorrow drives one from God. This need not happen, however.

A better way to handle such a crisis is to immediately confess the sin to Christ and move back into relationship with Him, by faith in His forgiving grace. First John 1:9 says, "If we confess our sins, he is faithful and just and will forgive us our sins and purify us from all unrighteousness." An Old Testament promise concerning God is helpful for us. Second Samuel 14:14 reads: "God does not take away life; instead, he devises ways so that a banished person may not remain estranged from him."

Such a crisis does not forfeit or negate all the previous relationship and growth that has occurred in the spiritual life. Indeed, a deep trust in the scriptures here quoted would lead us to believe that with such confession and immediate return to the relationship we have with the Lord, our walk with God picks up again at that point. Every experience of sin, and its consequent forgiveness, teaches us something about the love and grace of God. We need to remember that God does not want any person to be estranged from His love and forgiveness. "He is patient with you, not wanting anyone to perish, but everyone to come to repentance" (2 Peter 3:9).

Now some will wonder if God's grace and His ready forgiveness would not make sinning too easy. Would this "quick forgiveness" encourage a man to develop a careless cycle of sinning and asking forgiveness? No! The relationship of which we're talking in the sanctified life is maintained by love—love on God's part and love on the human side. And love that would take advantage of the Father's grace and mercy would soon be suspect. It would not have the fervor necesssary to maintain a sustained relationship with Christ.

What troubles us about this is our own inability to see this divine/human transaction take place, because we see sin as requiring punishment. But the punishment for sin has been dealt with by God, on a cross. Let us remember that Christ is more interested in purification than in punishment. Hence, His willingness to plead our case before our Father, because as long as a man stays out of relationship with Christ, sin has opportunity to establish dominion. God's desire is that men may have victory over sin. Forgiveness and bringing man back into relationship with Him is God's way of achieving such victory.

So, immediate confession and moving right back into relationship, resuming the walk in the Spirit, is the remedy for sin—wherever and whenever it occurs.

Huber L. Drumwright, in his book *Prayer Rediscovered*, writes, "To be strengthened in the inner man is to allow the Holy Spirit to have his way in the individual's life. Inner strengthening comes only through the Holy Spirit; but, thanks be to God, there is no short supply of divine energy."[1] The Christian's safety is to confess his sin immediately and allow the divine energy of God's forgiveness and cleansing to restore and reconcile.

Someone may ask if such confession should be brought to the altar in a public service. If that is a convenient time, and you feel comfortable with that, yes. But it is not necessary! Why wait for a time to elapse, when you could be quickly back into relationship? I submit that the privilege of the "priesthood of all believers" be exercised. God, through Jesus Christ, gives us the privilege of calling on the Advocate of our soul, Jesus Christ, immediately. We can transact divine business at the moment we become aware that we have committed the sin.

Someone has said that "Christianity is not a list of practices, but a close and vital relationship with Christ." He is right! And where the heart centers its affections on Christ, and chooses that love at all cost, a close relationship results. And the benefit of such a relationship is a continued cleansing.

Here, then, is the remedy for sin. But Paul tells us how to avoid the crisis to begin with. We need to heed his word: "Since, then, you have been raised with Christ, set your hearts on things above, where Christ is seated at the right hand of God. Set your minds on things above, not on earthly things. For you died, and your life is now hidden with Christ in God" (Colossians 3:1-3).

The writer of the Epistle to the Hebrews gives us this advice: "Let us fix our eyes on Jesus, the author and perfecter of our faith" (12:2). This is our safesy way to walk in the Spirit.

Chapter 9

Don't Expect Too Much!

It seems like a contradiction to warn you not to expect too much after I have encouraged you to believe that holy living is possible. You *can* expect much from God and never be disappointed. But do not expect to accomplish anything *in your own power.* Sometimes we expect too much out of ourselves and too much out of the sanctified life. Let me explain.

Some have thought that in the sanctified life it would be impossible to sin. They view the sanctified relationship—the separated life, the set-apart heart—as being incapable of sinning. If sin is removed from the heart, they say, then how can one sin?

The possibility is the same as it was with Adam. The power of choice still exists. Committing sin is always a possibility. Scripture reminds us that "your enemy the devil prowls around like a roaring lion looking for someone to devour" (1 Peter 5:8). This means that even the sanctified are not exempt from Satan's designs.

Anytime the focus of the heart is taken off Christ, the possibility of sinning is great. It is good to remember that the sanctified life does not elevate a man above sin. It does give him the strength and inner will to resist its temptation. But it is God's power and strength, not our own. That's why we should not rely on our strength or expect too much from the human side. We are weak and our humanness is no match for Satan. Our sufficiency is of God!

The sanctified life needs the same intensity that it exercised before consecration. Here is where some fail. After they are sanctified they slack off on their devotional life. This makes them vulnerable to Satan's attack. Sanctification does not equip us to be more self-sufficient. It puts us under the control of the Spirit, whose inner resources are our strength.

Mistakes or Sins

Another error sometimes expressed in regard to the sanctified life is the confusion between error or mistakes, and sin. Here is where a definition of *sin* is helpful. In the New Testament *hamartia* is the Greek word most often used to express sin and means "missing of the mark." But the deeper word *adakia* means iniquity and carries the idea of transgression. It is the intent of the sinful heart to deliberately break the laws of God. The Scriptures' conclusion for the willful-wayward is, "Anyone, then, who knows the good he ought to do and doesn't do it, sins" (James 4:17). As we have said earlier, sin is a wilful transgression of a known law of God.

One can quickly distinguish sin from an error or a mistake. An error or mistake is unintentional and done without any thought or motive for wrongdoing. While there is often regret for such errors and mistakes, they are not sins.

What we need to remember in our sanctified relationship is that God judges us on the basis of our *motive*. He is not waiting like some tyrant to catch us up in some wrongdoing. He is waiting, with mercy, to teach us "the most excellent way" (1 Corinthians 12:31).

Keeping Power

Another area where we may expect too much in the sanctified life is to believe that all of life will now run smoothly, with no problems, no failures, no valleys.

God has not promised such blessing for the sanctified. He has promised victory in the midst of defeat, His presence in the midst of valleys, and guidance for the problem times. God's sustaining grace and keeping power are greater blessings than a life free from any hard moments. Isaiah echoed God's promise to His followers when he wrote: "Fear not, for I have redeemed you; I have called you by name; you are mine. When you pass through the waters, I will be with you; and when you pass through the rivers, they will not sweep over you. When you walk through the fire, you will not be burned, the flames will not set you ablaze. For I am the Lord, your God" (Isaiah 43:1-3).

Understanding Our Humanness

There is another subject that needs highlighting. Be careful that your sanctified "halo" does not become a hindrance. That's right! If you polish your sanctified "halo" and see yourself as a saint, it's going to be a hindrance to those with whom you associate and attempt to share. Don't expect too much of yourself!

The sanctified man is still an "earthen vessel." He is recipient of God's saving and sanctifying grace, but he is still a pilgrim in a world where humanness is a fact. Any air of superiority or spiritual pride threatens the very relationship we so treasure. We need to remember that the relationship we have in the sanctified life is knit in love, and the object of our love is Christ. When we realize the price for such a relationship, we "pour contempt on all [our] pride," and are humbled that He should love such as we.

Temptation

We need to say a word, as well, about temptation. Temptation will always be companion to man on his spiritual pilgrimage. But understand, first, that temptation *is not* sin. The Scriptures say: "We do not have a high priest who is unable to sympathize with our weaknesses, but we have one who has been tempted in every way, just as we are—yet was without sin" (Hebrews 4:15).

Our Lord was tempted. So, likewise, we will face temptation. Temptation leads to sin *only* when the heart responds and the will yields to the temptation.

The "game plan" for victory over temptation is this: "Submit yourselves, then, to God. Resist the devil, and he will flee from you" (James 4:7). E. Stanley Jones has reminded us that "in temptation, flight is better than fight."

In temptation we need to distinguish between evil thoughts (sinful) and thoughts of evil (temptation). Often the two are confused and it causes discouragement in the Christian's walk. If we allow our minds to think on certain things, knowing that they are evil or will lead us to evil, we are inviting defeat. But, this is to be distinguished from those temptations that come upon, or invite our thoughts. If we give no need to them and do not submit to their begging, we have not sinned.

Encouragement for us in the moment of temptation is found in Paul's letters. He wrote to the Corinthians: "No temptation has seized you except what is common to man. And God is faithful; he will not let you be tempted beyond what you can bear. But when you are tempted, he will also provide a way out so that you can stand up under it" (1 Corinthians 10:13).

Final Thoughts

Formula for Spiritual Fitness
(S-A-F-E-T-Y)
  S — State the Problem
  A — Ask for Wisdom
  F — Feed the Heart with the Word
  E — Ease the Mind (Rest, Psalm 37)
  T — Think Victory!
  Y — Yield to the Guidance/Control of the Holy Spirit
  This is the victory! Charles Wesley puts it well in a hymn:

> *My chains fell off,*
>   *My heart was free.*
> *I rose, went forth*
>   *And followed thee!"*

And so can you!

Reference Notes

CHAPTER 1

1. W. E. Sangster, *The Path to Perfection* (New York: Abingdon-Cokesbury Press, 1943), 37-52. (Names of books are spelled out for clarity.)

2. Paul S. Rees, "Holiness, Holy," Everett F. Harrison, ed., *Baker's Dictionary of Theology* (Grand Rapids: Baker Book House, 1960), 269.

3. Wesley Tracy, *When Adam Clarke Preached, People Listened* (Kansas City: Beacon Hill Press of Kansas City, 1981), 119-20.

4. Ibid.

5. Lowell Peacock, *Quote, Unquote,* Lloyd Cory, Comp. (Wheaton, Ill.: Victor Books, 1977), 23-24.

CHAPTER 2

1. Edward R. Dayton, *Tools for Time Management* (Grand Rapids: Zondervan Publishing House, 1974), 81.

2. Milo L. Arnold, *The Christian Adventure* (Kansas City: Beacon Hill Press of Kansas City, 1974), 10.

3. Terry C. Muck, "10 Questions About the Devotional Life" *(Leadership,* Vol. III, No. 1, 1982), 36.

CHAPTER 3

1. John T. Seamands, *Tell It Well: Communicating the Gospel Across Cultures* (Kansas City: Beacon Hill Press of Kansas City, 1981), 125.

2. Cf. Vance Havner, *Pepper 'n Salt* (Westwood, N.J.: Fleming H. Revell Co., 1966), 49.

CHAPTER 4

1. Pauline E. Spray, *Coping with Tension* (Grand Rapids: Baker Book House, 1981), 81.

2. Tracy, *When Adam Clarke Preached,* 181.

3. *Leadership,* 35.

4. Keith W. Sehnert, *Stress/Unstress* (Minneapolis: Augsburg Publishing House, 1981), 193.

CHAPTER 5

1. E. Stanley Jones, *The Word Became Flesh* (Nashville: Abingdon Press, 1963), 355.

2. Hannah Whitall Smith, *The Christian's Secret of a Happy Life* (Old Tappan, N.J.: Spire Books, 1942), 149.

CHAPTER 6

1. Oswald Chambers, quoted by Harold L. Myra in *Leadership*, 55.

2. Charlie W. Shedd, *Getting Through to the Wonderful You* (Old Tappan, N.J.: Fleming H. Revell Co., 1976), 94.

3. Huber L. Drumwright, *Prayer Rediscovered* (Nashville: Broadman Press, 1978), 148.

4. Rufus Jones, quoted by Pauline E. Spray in *Coping with Tension*, 37.

CHAPTER 7

1. A. W. Tozer, quoted by Bill Bright in "Getting to Know God," *Tough Questions; Christian Answers* (Kansas City: Beacon Hill Press of Kansas City, 1981), 6-7.

2. Hal Lindsey, *The Guilt Trip* (Grand Rapids: Zondervan Publishing House, 1972), 7.

3. John Seamands, *Tell It Well*, 11.

4. Hannah Whitall Smith, *Every Day Religion* (New York: Fleming H. Revell Co., 1893), 180.

CHAPTER 8

1. Drumwright, *Prayer Rediscovered*, 101.